First published in Great Britain in 2004 by
Virgin Books Ltd
Thames Wharf Studios
Rainville Road
London
W6 9HA

A catalogue record for this book is available from the
British Library.

ISBN 1 85227 235 X

Busted managed by Richard Rashman and
Matt Fletcher for Prestige Management.

Art direction by Paul West at Form®
(www.form.uk.com)
Designed by Andy Harvey at Form®

Printed by The Bath Press.

Photographs:

James McMillan: 2-3, 8, 10-11, 12, 13, 14 (T-R), 15, 17
(T-R, B), 19, 21 (B), 22, 23, 25, 28, 29 (T-L, T-M, B), 30-31,
32-33, 39, 40, 41, 42, 43, 44, 45, 49, 51 (T-R), 52-53, 55, 56,
57, 58, 59, 61, 62, 63 (T-R), 64, 67, 69, 70, 71, 73, 74-75, 76-77

Ellis Parrinder at PCP Agency: 5, 7, 9, 14 (T-L), 17 (T-L),
21 (T), 27, 31,32, 47, 48, 63 (B)

Dean Chalkley/Idols Licensing and Publicity
Limited: 51 (T-L)

Antony Cutajar/Idols Licensing and Publicity
Limited: 18

Guy Heritage/Idols Licensing and Publicity
Limited: 24, 26, 34, 35, 36, 79

Tracey Griffin/Idols Licensing and Publicity
Limited: 29 (T-R)

David Tonge/Idols Licensing and Publicity
Limited: 16

David Titlow/Idols Licensing and Publicity
Limited: 63 (T-L)

Con-
tents

Introduc-tion

When I was first asked how I felt about spending one month on the road with the most exciting British pop group of the last five years, I said one thing: 'Haven't the Fast Food Rockers split up?'

Two weeks later I was on the Busted tour bus. With unrestricted access to the band for an entire month I found myself at the centre of the Busted whirlwind: the fan pandemonium, the 24 dates, the eight cities, the quarter of a million tickets sold, and the depressing sight of one young musician's descent into full-blown soft-cheese addiction.

'Just make us look cool,' James said, echoing a line in the movie *Almost Famous*, where a rock group are joined on the road by a journalist.

'Stop nicking lines out of films,' I said.

'Well, just write what happens, then,' he said, and that was that.

So here it is – a book about what it's really like to be on the road with one of the biggest pop groups in Britain. In one word, it's fun. But one word wouldn't make for much of a book, so read on for your very own Access All Areas pass. Just don't stand underneath any hotel windows when Matt's holding a TV.

Peter Robinson
London, April 2004

Rehear-sals

London Docklands Arena, 24 February 2004. Three o'clock in the afternoon. At the edge of the stage, James's bag is on fire. 'My bag is on fire,' he notes. 'Is that supposed to happen?'

It is not supposed to happen – James's bag is the unfortunate casualty of one pyrotechnic unexpectedly deciding to explode itself – but that is why the band are here today, in this empty arena, ironing out the creases and putting the finishing touches to their biggest live show to date. For one month Busted have been holed up at John Henry's rehearsal complex in north London – later today Charlie will admit that this has been the nearest he's ever come to a nine-to-five job – but today is their first opportunity to run through the show in the sort of venue they'll be playing for real.

James crosses the stage, stomps on his bag to put out the flames and examines the smouldering remains. The nylon has melted and the zip is stuck shut. He'll be needing a new bag for the tour.

Tickets first went on sale almost a year ago, before the band's first album, *Busted*, sold its millionth copy and long before their second album, *A Present For Everyone*, sold as many copies in its first three weeks as *Busted* did in its entire chart run. In the time since

last spring's national theatre tour, Busted have gone from being the brightest hopes on the pop block to household names, and are arguably the biggest pop band in the country. To begin with, only seven dates were announced for this tour; when they began selling out, more dates were added. And then *more* dates were added. Eventually the *A Ticket For Everyone* tour had notched up 24 sold-out arena dates.

The boys have been deep in preparation for the tour, and their priorities are as straight as ever. No bags have been packed, but James and Charlie have been feverishly loading songs into their respective iPods. Matt, meanwhile, has simply thrown all his CDs into a bag and will drag them with him from venue to venue.

Over a takeaway lunch, the band take one final look over the set list. Right now, it looks like this: 'Air Hostess', 'That Thing You Do', 'What I Go To School For', 'She Wants To Be Me', '3am', 'Why', 'Loner In Love', 'Who's David', 'Teenage Kicks', 'Better Than This', then a sequence in which Charlie will perform a drum solo, followed by a cover of Black Eyed Peas' 'Where Is The Love?', 'Fake', 'Nerdy' and 'You Said No'. The encore will consist of three songs: 'Year 3000', 'Sleeping With The Light On' and finally 'Crashed

0000 240304

ATFE

CTW 101003

★★★

Aeroporto

VIA Dublin/
Belfast/
Newcastle/
Nottingham/
Birmingham/
Sheffield/
Cardiff/
London/
Glasgow/
Manchester/

★★★

BSTD

DESTINATION

BUSTED

Rehearsals

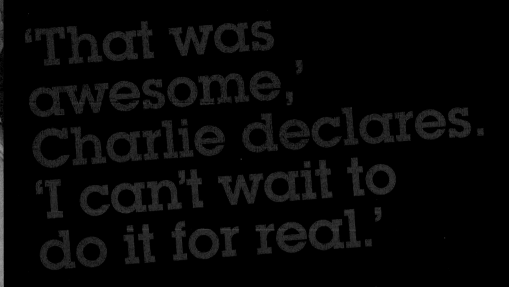

'That was awesome,' Charlie declares. 'I can't wait to do it for real.'

The Wedding', at the end of which the band will each jump through a hole in the stage and disappear from view.

'We totally knew from the word go that "Air Hostess" had to be the opening track,' Matt explains. 'If only because of the amazing "Do do do do do do" intro. From that point onwards we had to place our singles strategically throughout the set, and then pick out which album tracks and B-sides we wanted to play. What's great is that when we're doing them live, some of the album tracks, like "3am", sound just as good as the singles.'

'It's great to feel the show coming together,' Charlie agrees. He admits now that, on Busted's first tour, 'We really didn't have a clue what we were doing. The learning curve was unbelievably steep. This time it seems we're more on top of things.' James nods. 'I look back on the theatre tour and I think that it didn't really sound that good,' he adds, 'and this is our chance to make everything sound brilliant. Also, of course, we've got twice as much material now so there's no weak point in the set, whereas on the first tour I think we were a bit stuck for a few songs to play.'

Milling around today are some faces we'll be seeing a lot of over the next month. Up on the stage are the three extra musicians who'll be joining James, Matt and Charlie on stage each night: drummer Damon, keyboardist (and occasional bassist) Chris Banks and third guitarist Chris Leonard. Chatting in the corner are Busted's management team, Matt Fletcher (Fletch, to avoid confusion) and Richard Rashman, and, with a woolly hat pulled down over his face and a mobile phone clamped to his ear, we also find Adam Lambert, Busted's tour manager. Adam's job is to make sure things happen when the schedule says they should happen; without Adam the tour simply wouldn't happen at all.

After lunch the stage is cleared and the band run through the gig, in full, for the very first time. It's a spectacular show, from the moment the boys magically appear from below the stage for 'Air Hostess' to the final, screeching feedback of the last few seconds of 'Crashed The Wedding', and it captures perfectly everything which makes Busted Britain's most innovative pop band. Afterwards, the boys are ecstatic. 'That was awesome,' Charlie declares. 'I can't wait to do it for real.'

He won't have to wait long – in two days we'll be in Dublin for the first night.

Dublin

February 26

The band's white, double-level tour bus is waiting outside the hotel, chugging and ready to go. Having checked into his room, Charlie is the first to emerge from the hotel's glass revolving doors – big, green coat, hat pulled down over his eyes, sandwich in hand, ready for action. He jumps on the bus and takes a look around: at the wood-effect sideboards, the well-stocked fruit bowl, the on-board toilet (into which, Charlie insists, there will be deposited no solids), the plump leather seats. 'This,' he declares, dropping some sandwich on the carpet, 'is a nice tour bus.'

It's just as well. For Charlie, Matt and James this bus will be the nearest thing to home over the next month, as they visit ten cities around the British Isles. Charlie's obviously excited at the prospect of going on tour, and bounds up the steep stairwell to check out the bunks and second seating area. 'It's more a case of it being a nice, and rather large, taxi,' he decides. 'A taxi in which you can sometimes sleep. I always get a good sleep on tour buses.'

Before long James and – only a little late – Matt join us on the bus, the door slides itself shut and we begin our journey to Dublin's Point Depot, the scene for tonight and tomorrow's gigs. Time for more exploration, this time with the whole band clambering around the bus. It is swiftly established that one of the seats in the upstairs lounge will be, in Matt's words, 'the captain's chair'.

'This,' he says, 'is where the referee sits when we are playing Connect 4.' It is worth noting that, if you believe Connect 4 to be a game that requires no referee, you have never experienced the heated arguments that occur when Matt and Charlie are playing. A paperback copy of *Killing Pablo* ('the hunt for the richest, most powerful criminal in history', apparently) lies unread on the counter. Perhaps wisely, nobody admits ownership of the book.

After a twenty-minute drive, during which the boys carry out a full inspection of the tour bus minibar (some cans of Coke, some water and, for after the show, rather a lot of beer), we pull up at The Point, drive through a set of sturdy,

'This,' declares James, 'is our best video so far.'

fan-flanked gates and stop in the backstage parking area. Before the bus door opens, Adam Lambert opens his bag and pulls out a fistful of yellow, Access All Areas tour laminates, each with a name on the back. These will be given to every member of the Busted tour party, and they must not be lost. We pull them over our heads and troop through the stage door to Busted's dressing room.

On the dressing table, we find the following: one box of man-size Kleenex, two tubs of Toni & Guy hair product (one Funky Gum, one Shine-Glaze), one tub of VO5 Texturing Gum, one packet of cushioned plasters, one can of Elnette hairspray, one packet of Nurofen, some Revlon Colorstay foundation, a tube of Garnier 2-in-1 dandruff shampoo, some Radox shower gel, a tin of Sure For Men Active Response deodorant, a tube of Gillette shaving gel, a tub of Vaseline, a tube of Colgate Total Advance toothpaste, a tube of Berocca vitamin and mineral tablets, some effervescent double-action Vitamin C + Zinc tablets, a tube of Boots effervescent Echinacea, a packet of witch hazel and tea tree cleaning and toning wipes, three toothbrushes (all clearly marked James, Matt and Charlie), red Gillette razors marked Charlie and James, 24 Vocalzone throat lozenges

and six blue towels. These items – along with the band's requested rider – will be in the dressing room on every night of the tour.

Before long, it's time for the first soundcheck. This is a routine the band will go through for every date over the next month – playing tracks from the set to check everything's working both on stage and halfway back in the arena, on the sound desk where musical director Gareth Brown will be controlling what comes out of the PA. The band run through 'Air Hostess', 'She Wants To Be Me' and 'Crashed The Wedding'. Everyone seems happy, so Busted retire once again to their dressing room. Here they are handed a rough edit of the video to 'Air Hostess'. They'd filmed the video three weeks ago in between tour rehearsals, and the post-production – swapping green screens for footage of airport runways, and

so on – is still in progress back in London. At one point, when an exterior shot shows the plane spinning 360° in the sky, the screen goes completely black, except for the words 'PLANE 360' spinning around.

'We should keep it like that,' Matt announces. 'It would be the world's cheapest special effect.'

'This,' declares James, 'is our best video so far.'

It is agreed that 'Air Hostess' is certainly better than the video for 'Who's David', mention of which prompts a series of groans from the band. It was boring, says Charlie. It featured female acrobats for no reason whatsoever, adds Matt, who also suffered the ignominy of having to use the same phone box in the 'Who's David' video as in the 'Sleeping With The Light On' clip. 'It did rather seem as if someone

'Listen to that,'
Matt grins.
'They're going
to be screaming
for us later.'

had decided that, whenever Busted do a song which isn't about air hostesses getting off with teachers at a wedding in the year 3000, I have to stand looking pensive in a phone box,' he adds. 'Not just a phone box. The phone box. The Matt From Busted Phone Box Of Moodiness.'

Another part of the daily on-the-road routine is catering. Catering is where dinner happens. But dinner is not called dinner, it is called catering. The boys decide to go for catering at 6 p.m., half an hour before the doors open.

During the first course, James pauses and stares at Matt.

James: Matt, you're eating very weirdly today.

Matt: How?

James: I don't know. It's just your *mouth*. It's weird.

Charlie: I don't like this soup.

James: What is it?

Charlie: Potato and leek.

Matt: But you don't like leek.

Charlie: Yeah, I know.

Matt: I don't eat weirdly, do I?

At 7.30 p.m. we hear the first screams of the tour: the warm up is beginning. 'Listen to that.' Matt grins. 'They're going to be screaming for us later.'

While McFly are on stage, Busted are getting ready in their dressing room and there's a moment, a couple of minutes before the band make their way to the stage, when Charlie's regular nonchalant persona slips slightly to reveal an 18-year-old musician thrilled at the idea of going on stage. Any first-night nerves seem to have been superseded by a feeling of utter exhilaration, and from the moment the band first appear on stage – to an audience response Matt will later claim is among the loudest of his career so far – they're in their element. The number '3am' is incendiary tonight, and Matt's solo spot establishes 'Better Than This' as an unexpected audience favourite.

After the show we pause for a short while in the dressing room then grab our stuff, jump back onto the tour bus and drive back to the hotel to freshen up before heading out on the town. There's another gig tomorrow night, but the band agree to allow themselves a few drinks in a swank club called Lily's Bordello – which sounds rather more outré than it actually is, and is well known in rock and pop circles as the ideal destination for an after-show drink. By 1 a.m. the drink is flowing freely and a toast is made to the first date of the tour.

Then Bono from U2 arrives, and we have to give him our seats.

Dublin

On the tour bus, James is in a bad mood. Flicking through a car magazine two months ago he had seen a Delorean – the exact model used in the original *Back To The Future* films, with the doors that flap up in the air like wings – for sale, but hesitated about buying it on two grounds. Firstly, he still hasn't passed his driving test. Secondly, the house he was living in at the time didn't have a garage or even a parking space and James felt that leaving a time machine like one in a film he'd seen sat on the roadside was slightly absurd. In the time since, he's bought a new house – with a parking space – but he's just heard that the Delorean has been sold. 'Those cars,' he mopes, 'are as rare as rocking-horses***. I don't want a Porsche, and I will not be getting an X5. Deloreans are a far more elite car than that.'

Are they practical?

'No, not at all. I'm not a very practical person. But when I watched *Back To The Future* again the other day I suddenly realised that Deloreans were the reason I'd wanted to drive. Literally, the *only* reason.'

From the stairwell, Matt points out that James seems not to have taken into account the fact that the Delorean he eventually buys will, in all likelihood, have difficulty travelling through time.

'I know,' James says, a little unhappily. 'I know this. But as long as those doors spring up and I can dress it up to make it look like the one in the film, I'll be happy. I'll get some smoke machines put in the back.'

Why don't you get a Tannoy installed on the top, someone suggests, so you can drive around going, 'Look, I'm James out of Busted and I'm driving the car from *Back To The Future*'?

'Perhaps. It would be so cool to go back down to Southend and to drive down the road with the film soundtrack blaring out of the window. So next time I see one I'm going to buy it, park it in my new parking space, and leave it there until I can drive it.'

'In typical James fashion,' Matt snorts, 'the first things he moved into the house were his platinum discs.' James shrugs his shoulders and pulls one of his trademark well-you've-got-to-haven't-you-really expressions.

'I think what you should do in your house is knock the stairs down,' Fletch helpfully chirps, 'and get a fireman's pole.'

'Robbie Williams had a fireman's pole,' James retorts, and the topic is closed.

As the band's rider is laid out in the dressing room, Matt reflects on the first night's show and how it differed from playing to much smaller audiences on last year's theatre tour.

'I didn't expect it to be so different,' he admits. 'It seems much harder to connect with an audience on this scale. And then of course you feel like you're *trying* to connect with them, when you shouldn't be trying to do anything other than what comes naturally.' Still, he adds, it seems to be going all right so far. 'To get people so far back as involved as the people at the front is a real challenge, but people right at the back and up the sides often seem to get into the show much more than the people at the front.'

During tonight's show, and despite another thorough soundcheck, there is a repeat of some niggling problems from last night. Occasionally guitars will cut out during songs, and some of the guitars that have been tuned before the show have become mysteriously out-of-tune by the time they go on stage. It is agreed that this must be sorted out before tomorrow night's show in Belfast.

On the way back to the hotel we stop off at a service station for some supplies and everyone piles off the bus. As ever with Busted, the

'Look, I'm James out of Busted and I'm driving the [car from Back to the Future...]

escapade takes twice as long as is strictly necessary. Matt refuses to leave until he has inspected the CD rack which, as is often the case in petrol stations, stocks nothing but mid-price CD compilations aimed at people who spend a lot of their time driving, alone, on long, dark motorways. He flicks his way through the CDs – *20 Truckin' Hits*, *Keep On Truckin'* and so on – and for a brief moment looks as if he is considering making a purchase.

Back at the hotel the boys have three drinks in the bar before calling it a night and heading off to bed. Tomorrow we will leave early to travel to Belfast, check in to another hotel, and do this all over again. Adam explains that 'leaving early' seems to mean a 1 p.m. wake-up call for the band.

'I think,' Matt announces as he stops the lift doors from sliding shut, 'that I could get used to that sort of early start.' And he heads back to the bar.

Belfast

Matt flings the door open and waves his still uneaten steak around on a fork.

Snow lines the ground outside Belfast's Culloden Hotel, but the sun is shining. Down the road local kids are so bored that they're on a petrol station forecourt breathing in the compressed air, and outside the hotel a group of fans have written 'Busted rock' in the snow. But Busted are not the hotel's only special guests this weekend. One couple have chosen the hotel to host their wedding reception, and in the toilet two of the groom's friends discuss the pop stars who have – and there are various unamusing comments made about this over the course of the next two days – crashed the wedding.

'I'm a closet fan,' says one.

'I've never heard of them,' says the other, as he splashes his shoe.

While the band sign autographs for some waiting fans in reception, the wedding guests – one of whom Matt will later identify as having sported 'the very worst haircut of all time' – mill around and get drunk.

Hung over and hungry, Matt brings his room-service lunch – a massive steak – onto the bus, complete with china plate and sterling-silver cutlery. After two bites he pronounces himself full and casts the plate aside, virtually untouched.

We arrive at Belfast's Odyssey Arena at 4 p.m. As the bus drives through the electronic gates and past a group of fifty or so fans, Matt flings the door open and waves his still uneaten steak around on a fork. 'Who wants some of my meat?' he bellows, prompting a massive scream.

I mention that on the Internet auction site eBay right now someone is offering what they claim to be 'Busted soap' – a bar of Imperial Leather purportedly salvaged from a hotel room used by the band. A little disconcertingly, the seller promises that the soap comes 'with one hair attached'. There have already been three bids. Matt, for once, is speechless.

This afternoon's soundcheck is another opportunity to iron out the problems of the first two nights' shows, principally involving Charlie's guitar, which has developed a habit of cutting out during 'What I Go To School For'. Everything seems to be in order by 7.30 p.m. and, as Charlie and Damon practise their drum-off in the corner, the atmosphere in the dressing room is beginning to build once again.

Throughout the afternoon, staff at the Arena have painstakingly flyered each and every one of the 10,000 seats with a slip of paper informing audience members that under no circumstances are they to stand up during the performance. Charlie has already branded the rule 'utter bollocks' and on stage, after 'What I Go To School For', James addresses the issue. 'It's nice,' he begins, 'to see so many people standing up.' In the audience, confusion reigns. Some fans see this as permission to leave their seats; others, who've ignored the requests of the Arena and are already standing up, think it is a hint to sit down. 'Stand up!' James eventually shouts.

Not everything goes so smoothly. The problems with Charlie's guitar in 'What I Go To School For' have been solved tonight, but have been replaced by many more hitches. During 'Teenage Kicks', James's own guitar malfunctions so badly in the first verse that he has to run off stage for a replacement, leaving Matt to fill in his lines, and James only makes it back to his microphone in time for Charlie's verse. Similar problems plague the rest of the show, and in the four minutes between 'You Said No' and the encore the band are fuming.

After the show they storm through the corridor and shut themselves in their dressing room. This is Busted being Not At All Happy. Through the closed door you can make out James muttering something about how Formula One drivers don't have to sit in the pit for three minutes

waiting for their tyres to be changed. Charlie is swearing a lot. (Though, to be fair, Charlie is always swearing a lot.) To make matters even worse, tonight's has been the first show to be watched by the support acts, and Busted feel they've embarrassed themselves in front of their support acts. From behind the door a series of complaints are hurled around for fifteen minutes, but when the door opens, the situation has been diffused. At least, someone optimistically suggests, it's not the same show every night.

'Why couldn't it have been as good as last night?' Matt wonders, open palmed.

There is silence for thirty seconds, until Charlie finally answers, in typically playful Charlie manner: 'Well actually, I thought last night was shit.'

Back at the hotel, the wedding party, which has been here all afternoon and now all evening, is generously lubricated. Matt goes to his room to get changed and calm his nerves – his sixteen-year-old sister watched tonight's show, and will soon be introducing him to her new boyfriend for the first time – and when he returns he is immediately collared by the bride, who broadcasts the fact that she is 'more nervous about meeting Busted than

'Why couldn't it have been as good as last night?' Matt wonders, open palmed.

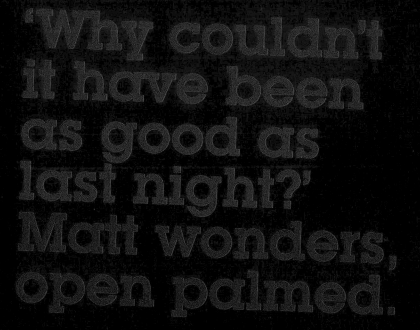

I was about getting married'. She goes on to thank Matt for making her day. Which, as Matt will later observe, is a rum old statement to make on your wedding day.

After a short spell at the bar, Adam persuades the hotel manager to open up a function room for the Busted party. The manager reluctantly shows us into a special room, but warns us that we must not

make a mess and must not spill any drinks, since the room has already been set for something very important tomorrow morning. This noted, James sets about spraying the room with champagne, because that is what rock stars – and Formula One drivers whose tyres have been changed quickly enough – sometimes do. The champagne has barely settled on the tablecloths, luxurious shag pile

and assembled members of the Busted touring crew before the manager storms back in and gives James an unceremonious bollocking in front of everyone. Against James's wishes, the ground refuses to open up and swallow him.

At 3.30 a.m., James invites us up to his room to listen to a new Busted song. This is one of those hotel rooms whose lights only work when a key card is inserted in a slot where the light switch should be. Having lost the appropriate card, James stumbles around in the dark, finds a knife and jams it in the hole. The lights come on – a happy consequence, seeing as the alternative was electrocution.

While he rummages through piles of caseless CDs and CD-less cases – none of which seem to correspond – he reflects on his champagne-related telling-off.

'It was only when we got in there that he said, "Oh, don't spill any drink." I was like, "C'mon, if you're partying in a room, then drinks are gonna get spilled." And that is exactly what happened.' Eventually James finds the CD he's looking for and slides it into the hotel room stereo. As it whirrs its way to the beginning of the song, he announces: 'This is one of the best songs Busted have ever recorded.'

The song – 'Thunderbirds Are Go' – will soundtrack the main title sequence of the forthcoming Hollywood version of the 1960s puppet show. At the end of last year the film's production company, Working Title (who've also worked on movies like *Love, Actually* and *Bridget Jones' Diary*) approached Busted with a view to recording a song for the film. They showed James, Matt and Charlie some rough footage from the movie

and the result is now blaring around James's hotel room, through an open window and out into the icy Belfast hill tops.

The spilled champagne is still playing on James's mind. 'Oh God.' He grimaces. 'The whole thing's just reminded me of when I was ten years old, and I bashed my friend's head against the wall at school.'

By accident?

'No, I was having a fight with him.' He laughs. 'But his mum was in the playground and just stood there yelling at me for ten minutes. I was sent to the head's office for further punishment and he was eating an apple. Every time he yelled something at me a little bit of apple hit me in the face.'

Belfast

Sunday afternoon on the tour bus.
Charlie and James nurse their
hangovers as Matt brews
some foul-smelling herbal tea that,
he tells us proudly, is the same
tea Madonna drinks when she's
on tour. James is wrestling with
the bus's built-in CD player.
'How does this work?' he wails.

'You leave it,' Matt retorts, 'to
someone who knows what they're
doing.' He presses the 'On' button
and the system springs to life. The
band listen to 'Thunderbirds Are Go'
twice. There are two different
versions – the fourteenth and
fifteenth reswizzles – on the CD,
which was sent direct from the
studio last week. On the fifteenth,
the guitars are a little higher in the
mix. After it has finished, Matt sits
in silence for a short while. 'I know
that this is the point when I'm
supposed to debate the merits of
both versions,' he says. 'I know I'm
supposed to say how much better
these versions sound than versions
eight and nine. But, to be quite
honest, I can't even tell the
difference. Is there a bit more
trumpet in it now? After a while,
he adds, 'I preferred the first mix.'

During the soundcheck at Odyssey
Arena, Charlie mistakenly lets
rip a cry of 'Hello Dublin!'

'Hello Spain!' yells James.

'Hello Reigate!' Charlie concludes.

The band play a bit of the Red Hot
Chili Peppers' 'Californication'.

Afterwards, they discuss last night's
problems, and the previous
night's problems, and the previous
night's problems, with Skirmish,
the tour's main guitar tech. Strings
keep breaking, Fletch contributes.
Shit happens, Skirmish shrugs.
I need a new guitar, James decides.
One of the guitar pedals is too
far away from the mic stand, Charlie
adds. The guitars keep going out
of tune for 'Teenage Kicks', Matt
notes. The problems are noted and
the band return to their PlayStation.

In spite of last night's stand-up
protest, the venue staff have once
again flyered each seat with strict
instructions for the audience to
remain seated. Nonetheless,
Busted's show tonight is the best
so far – the problems experienced
last night and in Dublin have been
solved, and the result is a massive
boost to the band's confidence
that makes, for the first time, for
a blazing live show.

Tonight is also the first time
the entire A Ticket For Everyone
entourage share the same hotel bar
drinks. All three bands sit in a large
circle and drinks flow until 3 a.m.
It is just as well, Richard Rashman
notes, that tomorrow is a day off.

The next time we see each other,
we'll all be in Newcastle.

During the soundcheck at Odyssey Arena, Charlie mistakenly lets rip a cry of 'Hello Dublin!'

'If you're going to break a guitar, break a guitar spectacularly,' James advises.

miming because your hands didn't even change position on your guitar." It's, like, that's because all of our songs are written on three chords – the reasons my hands don't move is because I'm only moving one finger to drop the chord down to a D, then moving two fingers down a string to get to a C. So people criticise our ability to play music when they clearly can't hear how it was written – or even how it should look when it's played live – so I don't get too worked up about it.'

Wouldn't you say that there's still a manufactured element to the way you were first presented, though? You were in school uniforms. You didn't wear them around the house, did you? Do you see how people still find it difficult to believe that as a band you aren't just as stylised now?

'The distinction which I think makes us a real band rather than a manufactured band is that we were a band before we had a record deal; we went round all the record labels playing songs we'd written ourselves, acoustically, and in the end we went for a record deal which wasn't offering the most money but one which was offering us the best opportunity to develop as artists and as songwriters. I'm not sure that on any of those counts there's a more credible way of having gone about any of it.' It's been noted that you would

probably have gained respect more quickly if you'd all been pig-ugly.

'Yeah.' James laughs. 'It's interesting. Everyone always goes, "Well, you're really successful because you look good," and I just say, "Name me an ugly star." How many ugly famous people can you think of? The most credible artists – Chris Martin from Coldplay, the Strokes, the White Stripes – these are all good-looking people. There are no ugly superstars.'

A crew from German pop magazine Bravo are here to shoot some behind-the-scenes pictures with the band. Germany is one of Busted's biggest markets outside the UK – so popular, in fact, that last year the German branch of Universal Records persuaded the band to record a frankly bizarre song called 'Hurra, Hurra, Die Schule Brennt' ('Hurrah, Hurrah, The School Is On Fire') as a single. The song is an old pop classic back in Germany, and lyrics go: 'Their lips are blue, hair is green, they got piercings in their ears / Sticking it out of pockets, some bottles of beer / They're running through the streets and every place that they go / Is a stench of fuel in the air'. Perhaps wisely the single was not elected for release as a UK single, though it did turn up as a 'Crashed The Wedding' B-side. Before the show, talk has turned to

the band's guitars. When they leave the stage at the end of the very final song, 'Crashed The Wedding', they run to the top of the stage set and jump through a hole in the floor and on to crash mats, but before they do that their guitars are placed very carefully on the floor. There has been some debate over whether there is any place for Being Very Careful in a rock show.

'If you're going to break a guitar, break a guitar spectacularly,' James advises. 'But if you're not going to break it, put it down carefully. You can't do it halfway. I like my guitar. Someone spent a lot of time making it, and I hate waste.'

'Yes, you see that's the problem,' Charlie agrees. 'It's the fact that I have a nice guitar and I don't want to break it.'

'I don't think anyone's suggesting we drive over our guitars in a steamroller,' Matt says. 'But we could just sort of...drop them on the stage. So it looks a bit less like we're working in a museum.'

'But I'd rather just put mine down,' Charlie says. 'I do have the best guitar.'

'Shame you don't know how to play it,' James teases.

'Yeah,' Matt says, guffawing, 'and that you've got a small penis.'

teen pop magazines have a far more relaxed approach to sex and will often feature full-frontal nudity and breathtakingly graphic cartoon strips among the posters of new pop acts, but even Matt is shocked about what he finds in *Loka*. Over two pages is a practical how-to guide concerning an eyebrow-raising sexual act that is still illegal in many parts of the world. 'Oh my goodness,' Matt shrieks. 'Oh. My. GOODNESS!'

Charlie: Ooh, a funny one...

Alvaro: How long have you ever been without a shower?

Matt: Did you know that James has been wearing those trousers every day on the tour, and they still haven't been washed?

James: But they don't smell.

Matt: THAT DOESN'T MEAN THEY'RE CLEAN!

Alvaro: Would you participate in *Pop Idol*?

All: No.

Alvaro: If you had three questions to ask a genie, what would they be?

Charlie: I'd ask to be able to fly, and to have eternal happiness...

Matt: But the problem there, Charlie, is that that is *pretend* happiness.

Charlie: It would be real though.

Matt: No it wouldn't! So, you'd wake up in bed one morning having been stabbed and you'd be like, 'I don't care because I'm so eternally happy'?

Charlie: Good point. Maybe I'd just go for having a really good immune system. Take the 'Happiness' off the list. I'll make *myself* happy, thank you very much.

Matt: Now you're wasting your genie!

The questions turn to sex, and the band are asked how old they were when they lost their respective virginities. 'So,' Matt says, turning to Alvaro, 'when did you lose *your* virginity?'

'When I was eighteen,' comes the reply.

'Eighteen?! I thought you were all supposed to be randy in Spain.' Matt flicks through one of Alvaro's magazines for evidence. In Europe,

'Yes,' Alvaro concedes, the evidence seemingly against him. 'I suppose I was quite late.'

With the interview over, Charlie confides that he has been experiencing some strange dreams while on tour. Recurring instances involve Charlie being shot, stabbed and electrocuted. 'The blood,' he moans, 'always feels really warm. The other night I dreamed I was in a cab going to my new house. There were some guys looking dodgy in the street and, as I handed a £20 note over to the cab driver, the window smashed and a gun was held to my face.'

What do you think that says about your life?

'That I'm scared of being held up at gunpoint while paying for a cab.'

'So,' begins the police constable with his notebook open, 'can one of you tell me exactly what happened?'

presence into even sharper contrast with the perky, fun-filled Busted of the 'What I Go To School For' era.

'I think that's good in a way,' Charlie announces. 'The further we go away from that the better. We're still energetic, we're just not so happy-clappy.'

'I didn't like tonight's show,' James suddenly says.

'It was great tonight,' Matt counters.

'Partly because there were loads of teenage blokes in the audience. I was looking at them thinking, I bet you lot pretend not to like Busted at college – but I know you bloody love us!'

As the long journey drags on, Charlie and James disappear upstairs for a game of Connect 4 while Matt, Fletch, physio Neil and James's brother Nick stay downstairs and watch *Phoenix Nights* on DVD. After what seems like an age, we arrive back at the hotel. Three days of late nights and hard work have taken their toll on most of the crew. The hotel bar is empty.

'Let's just have a quiet drink in the bar and go to bed,' Matt suggests.

Four hours later the intermittent flashing blue light of a parked police car illuminates the hotel bar. 'So,' begins the police officer with his notebook open, 'can one of you

tell me exactly what happened?'

'Well,' Matt begins. 'The idea was to have a quiet drink and then go to bed...'

But that's not exactly what happened. Flashback four hours: after the one quiet drink it strikes James and Matt that, with a day off from touring tomorrow, there is no real reason for the drinks to stop at one, or two; or even for those drinks to be particularly quiet.

The booze begins to escalate from pints of lager to shots of tequila and before long Matt is behind the hotel bar, harassing a member of the night staff. 'Where are your spirits?' Matt demands. 'Do you do Aftershock?' (Matt is referring to the bright red, syrupy booze only ever consumed by people who are already drunk.) 'Let me give you a hand. Where are your cigars?'

A short while later, having decided that the miraculous healing power of alcohol has cured his dodgy leg, Matt has found a pair of scissors and cut off the bandage on his knee. It lies in the ashtray.

As it becomes increasingly obvious that the night porter – who bears no resemblance whatsoever to a 70s cowboy-movie star but has been christened Clint Eastwood by Matt and James – is hoping to close the bar, we move up to Matt's bedroom, Room 420. A call to Clint Eastwood produces a tray bearing three pints of Stella and three double JD & Cokes, one of which is promptly spilled on the floor as Matt swings around brandishing one of the two remaining baseball caps from yesterday's hat spree. 'I'm going to distress it,' he announces, and sets about the peak with a pair of scissors. The finished item looks less like a customised fashion accessory than a £16.99 cap whose peak has been cut up by a pissed-up member of Busted, but Matt seems pleased with his handiwork and pulls the cap onto his head.

The window has been left open by the maid responsible for today's room service and before long the contents of Matt's fruit basket – two bananas and a handful of grapes – have been thrown from our fourth-floor location onto the street below. The room's litter bin is the next item

to go sailing through the night air. Matt and James pull back from the window and take a look around the room. Matt has not yet finished with the window.

In the corner of the room is a large wooden cabinet, and in it is a 24-inch hotel TV. Hotel televisions are massive things that don't work like proper televisions. They spring to life for no reason, informing you that someone's silver Lexus is blocking traffic in the car park and could it please be moved before it is towed away; they have secret late-night channels showing films of people kissing each other, and they are fine-tuned to show nothing else that anybody would really want to watch. This particular hotel television, Matt jokes, is going out of the window.

After reaching round both sides of the set and pulling it out of the shelf – and out of the plug socket – Matt staggers around the room, then heads over to the window. When he walks back into the centre of the room, he is sans television. Two seconds later, we hear a huge smash.

James looks rather surprised. He will later explain that until Matt returned from the window – looking a little surprised himself – it had looked like he was just having a laugh. We all peer from the hotel window. There's

a lot of glass, plastic and circuitry lining the pavement.

It is, we all decide, time to go for a walk. As we head for the revolving doors on the way out of the hotel, the following exchange takes place.

Concierge: Have you just thrown a television out of your window?

Matt: No.

Concierge: All right then.

It's now 4 a.m. and we're wandering the streets of Birmingham. Through an underpass, past a strand of shops. We turn right, down Ryland Street, and then right again, into Rosel Way. It's a dead end. We turn back, then right again, into another dead end. By 4.20 we're lost, and Matt is on the ground following an ill-advised piggyback. We walk for a while longer until at 4.45 a.m. James spots a landmark ahead of us: the remains of a TV set, splashed across the pavement. It seems we've found the hotel, but, as we turn the corner into the hotel car park, we also find a police car.

Fletch and Adam are in reception talking to a policeman.

'So,' begins the police constable with his notebook open, 'can one of you tell me exactly what happened?'

The thrust of Matt's defence is this: 'I was really drunk, I thought

I was being funny, and then it got out of hand and I was really stupid.'

In the cold light of a hotel bar at 5 a.m. on a Monday, it's difficult not to agree. The police officer walks back out to reception to discuss what has happened with the hotel manager. In situations like this, further action is at the discretion of the hotel and the police officer in question. Between them they decide not to take matters any further, but that doesn't stop them giving Matt a bit of a scare.

'Well, Mr Willis,' the policeman says as he comes back into the bar, 'I'm afraid I'm going to have to ask you to sign a confession.'

Matt looks gutted and then quite surprised when the 'form' placed in front of him is just a blank sheet of paper. And that, apart from a few sheepish glances exchanged between James, Matt and whichever idiot had been complaining in Matt's hotel room that his on-the-road book needed some excitement, is that.

Now it really is time for bed.

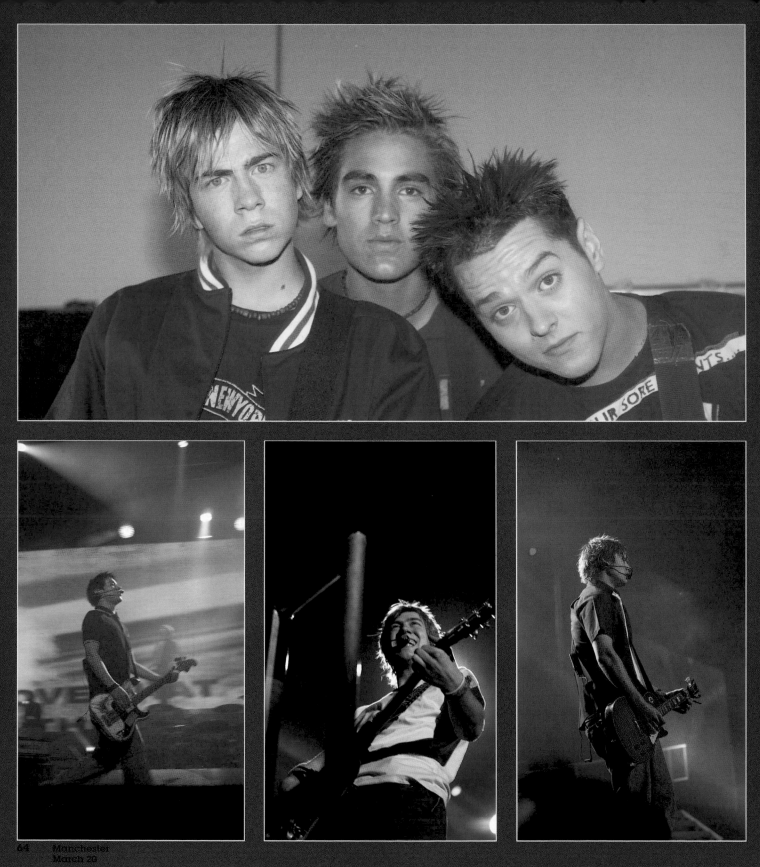

Man-chester

On DVD Day, Manchester is windy. So windy that, outside the arena, some fans are blown clean off their feet by an unexpected gust. In the dressing room, Matt is wearing the grey 'Punk Fakes' T-shirt – last seen when Busted were on the cover of the *Observer Music Monthly* magazine in a piece attempting to claim that, along with artists like the Sugababes, Busted were at the forefront of a new Britpop revolution. 'You won't be at all surprised to hear that my throat is buggered,' he moans. 'It was fine, and then it wasn't, and then it was fine again, and then...' He sprays something down his throat, and gags. 'That hasn't helped. I might as well have gone out and got really pissed last night for all the good a decent night's sleep has done.' He goes on to explain that the tour has already claimed another casualty: last night, in the hotel bar, Busted's press officer Heather had been attempting to recreate some boyband dance moves, managed to rupture a tendon in her leg and was last seen being stretchered out of the hotel and into the back of an ambulance.

It's time to shoot some backstage footage for the DVD, so everyone's ushered out of the dressing room for a short while. On the way out, Adam Lambert asks the cameraman whether he wants a guitar – which is on the coffee table along with a load of spent water bottles – in shot.

'Yeah,' says the cameraman. 'Let's have a bit of rock'n'roll.'

'Rock'n'roll.' Adam laughs. 'An acoustic guitar and some empty Evian bottles.'

McFly are just arriving, having only recently stepped off a plane from London, where they've been recording a performance for *CD:UK*. The wind, they say, was so bad that the turbulence was the worst any of them have ever experienced, and the pilot had to abandon one landing and try again. Two members of the band admit that they fully expected to die on the second attempt.

We walk out to inspect the arena and find a higher concentration of cameras than you'd get in your average *Big Brother* house – there are eleven attached to the front of the stage, all pointing at slightly different parts of the stage, and loads more have been positioned around the arena, which is freezing cold.

James, meanwhile, is telling Fletch and Richard about a guy he met in the hotel bar last night – an up-and-coming songwriter currently in a band called Dudefish. The name 'Dudefish' provokes some uncertain glances around the table. 'I think it's a cool name!' James protests. 'You're not going to forget it, are you. Ask me in two years the name of that guy's band, and I'll say, "The band's name was Dudefish."' James suggests that Fletch and Richard should meet the Dudefish dude, because his songs were really good.

'He likes the same bands as me, and he hates the same bands as me,' James continues. 'He played me some of his tracks – there was a great one called "I'm A Loser And A Clown".' I ask whether James sees a future for himself in artist management. He nods. 'Maybe. But there's a lot of other stuff I want to do first.'

Backstage before the gig, the dressing room is in pandemonium: assorted people from the band's label have dropped in with their kids to say hello, and Matt, Charlie and Fletch are having a meeting in the toilet. On emerging from his meeting Matt discovers that yesterday's Boursin has finally arrived, and begins to eat it out of the wrapper.

Showtime comes around quickly. Because it's being recorded, the lads' between-song banter is tempered slightly, and there's an awkward moment during Charlie's solo song 'Why' when his guitar fails. After the band have performed 'Fake', someone scuttles on stage from the wings and whispers something in James's ear. 'Now

London: Part Two

We're back at Wembley for the second series of London dates, and the final shows of the tour. Since we last saw the band they've played another Sheffield date and two in Birmingham, but there are three gigs to go this weekend – one tonight, one tomorrow and one on Sunday. The DVD and album have been recorded; anyone who's going to review the show has already been, and already it's feeling as if the tour is winding down, so the boys are more keen than ever not to let complacency set in. Not that they have much chance to rest on their laurels today – they'll be busy with another set of interviews, and at 5.30 p.m. there will be a private screening, in the boys' dressing room, of the *Thunderbirds* movie.

Charlie already has other things on his mind. Yesterday he picked up his new car, a vehicle so crammed with state-of-the-art gadgetry and gizmos that someone from the showroom spent yesterday morning showing Charlie how to work it. 'It's got all the Bluetooth stuff for my phone, and a TV, and lots of different electrical buttons,' Charlie enthuses, beaming. 'And it's got satellite navigation, which is amazing. Say I'm going to the Barfly in Glasgow. You type in "Barfly, Glasgow", and it takes you there. Which is good because I'm so shit at map reading.

The tyres are amazing. It's like driving a spaceship.'

What's it like driving a spaceship? 'Bloody cool.'

First up today is the soundcheck. Watching from the empty auditorium, a passing roadie notes with some amusement that, after a few weeks of dragging their heels during these afternoon run-throughs, Matt, James and Charlie seem genuinely to be enjoying their time on stage this afternoon.

In the dressing room it is mentioned that, this morning, tickets went on sale for the London dates of Madonna's 2004 tour. Concert ticket prices are all pretty steep these days, but Madonna's are unusually pricey, ranging from £50 to £160.

Charlie pokes his head around the bathroom door, toothbrush sticking out of his mouth, looking utterly appalled. 'Each?'

Yes.

'That's an absolute joke. I thought the same thing when the Rolling Stones played and their tickets were £150. Actually mine weren't because I got them cheaper. But that's not the point. You've got to see the full picture – perhaps they're doing it for tax reasons or something – but, if they're doing it just because they can, that's messed up. She's already got loads of money.'

How much would you pay to see Madonna?

'Three pounds. And that would have to include the booking fee. Fair dos to her and she's obviously good at what she does, but I really have no interest in anything she does.'

Also this week, James's brother Nick has been 'papped' for the first time, appearing in one of the tabloid papers with James in a record shop. Now, it's fair to say that Nick – who's appeared in the 'You Said No', 'Who's David' and 'Air Hostess' videos – doesn't mind having his face on camera, but he did find the experience a bit weird, especially since he says today that the first he knew of the picture being taken was when it actually turned up in the paper.

Matt has also been photographed recently – wandering down the street with a Sid Vicious poster – and has his own plans. 'I'm going to start a side project with a mate,' he confides as he munches on yet another packet of Boursin cheese. 'He's skint, so what we're going to do is set up some paparazzi shots of me doing things like falling over, buying some chips, breathing or whatever, and then he can flog them to magazines. He'll be minted!'

We mention the bar of eBay soap from earlier in the tour. By this point the auction has been mysteriously

the old videos, and having watched those what's good about this film is how true they've stayed to the characters. It's not a teen movie, it's not a "fifteen", it's a family movie. But you can count any number of family movies which are brilliant films.'

He counts about twelve and then gives up.

Tonight's show passes almost without incident. At one point, before 'She Wants To Be Me', Matt checks the set list and then pauses. 'I can't believe it's the third-to-last night of the tour,' he says, lauging, 'and I'm still checking the set list.' Before 'Britney', James follows his usual 'She's got diamonds on her titties' comment with '...in her new video', as if there is likely to be any suspicion in the audience's mind that Britney Spears wears a diamond breast adornment when she's putting the bins out. Towards the end of the song Matt and James miss their cues, sending Matt into fits of hysterics.

In tonight's jumping-through-a-hole-in-the-floor finale, Charlie manages to hit his head on the side of the stage. He is fine, but sees fit to turn the whole thing into a drama and insists on sympathy from everyone in the dressing room. 'You know,' Matt says afterwards, 'it's going to be weird playing small venues again.'

withdrawn, meaning that the winning bidders never received their Busted pube-and-soap parcel. But Matt has ideas for this, too. 'The plan is that I'm going to get all these little things signed by the band, and then the same mate can go off and sell them. It might as well be one of my friends who profits from it.'

At 7 p.m. Busted emerge from their

Thunderbirds screening. The boys had seen some rough cuts of the film last winter when they'd initially been approached to write the song, but this is the first time any of them had seen the whole thing, and it was an opportunity to see whether the film was any good. James seems happy.

'As soon as I heard we were doing the song I went out and bought all

March 28

After 24 dates, 10 cities, a quarter of a million tickets sold, 7 kilograms of Haribo, one broken television and countless minor injuries, the tour is finally over.

We jump in the Busted tour bus for one last time. It hasn't played host to this many people all tour – downstairs passengers spill from the seats, cram into the stairwell and even shut themselves in the toilet in an attempt to squeeze in; upstairs every bunk is full and the corridor is packed with people. As we sway our way through north London to the final after-show party, James reflects on the gig. 'I'm not really an "emotional last night" type of person,' he admits, 'but I enjoyed soaking up that feeling for one last time. As soon as I get out of bed tomorrow there will still be a million other things going on, and there'll be a million other things the day after that. But I'm never going to forget this tour.'

The bus grinds to a halt. We've arrived at our destination – the Eve club, on Regent Street in the heart of London. Eve is great for two reasons. Firstly because, in the 1960s, it was central to a massive Government sex scandal; secondly, and more importantly, because it has an illuminated dance floor.

Drink is free and the tunes are cheesy. 'Year 3000' packs the floor. Everyone dances. Some people fall over. One person bursts into tears. After 24 dates, 10 cities, a quarter of a million tickets sold, 7 kilograms of Haribo, one broken television and countless minor injuries, the tour is finally over.

At the end of the year, the band will do it all over again. Dates are already selling out for the band's 'A Ticket For Everyone Else' tour. In the corner of the dance floor, James mentions rumours he's heard that this tour will be the band's last. He laughs. 'The funny thing,' he shouts above the roar of OutKast's 'Hey Ya!', 'and the thing that some people don't realise, is that when we're on stage we have as good a time, if not a better time, than the fans do. That's just the way it is. If they want us here, we'll be here. We're not ready for a farewell tour. We haven't even really begun yet.'

As he staggers to his taxi, Matt has the very final word. 'This is what it's all been about,' he shouts. 'This is what being in Busted is ALL about. Playing live is everything.'

He falls into the cab.

Discog- raphy

WHAT I GO TO SCHOOL FOR
SINGLE PROMO

YOU SAID NO
SINGLE PROMO

WHAT I GO TO SCHOOL FOR
SINGLE CD1

16TH SEPTEMBER 2002
03

YOU SAID NO
SINGLE CD1

21ST APRIL 2003
01

WHAT I GO TO SCHOOL FOR
SINGLE CD2

16TH SEPTEMBER 2002
03

YOU SAID NO
SINGLE CD2

21ST APRIL 2003
01

BUSTED ALBUM
ALBUM

30TH SEPTEMBER 2002
01

SLEEPING WITH THE LIGHT ON
SINGLE PROMO

YEAR 3000
SINGLE PROMO

SLEEPING WITH THE LIGHT ON
SINGLE CD1

11TH AUGUST 2003
04

YEAR 3000
SINGLE CD1

13TH JANUARY 2003
02

SLEEPING WITH THE LIGHT ON
SINGLE CD2

11TH AUGUST 2003
04

YEAR 3000
SINGLE CD2

13TH JANUARY 2003
02

CRASHED THE WEDDING
SINGLE PROMO

CRASHED THE WEDDING
SINGLE CD1

10TH NOVEMBER 2003
01

CRASHED THE WEDDING
SINGLE CD2

10TH NOVEMBER 2003
01

A PRESENT FOR EVERYONE
ALBUM

17TH NOVEMBER 2003
02

WHO'S DAVID
SINGLE PROMO

WHO'S DAVID
SINGLE CD1

16TH FEBRUARY 2004
01

WHO'S DAVID
SINGLE CD2

16TH FEBRUARY 2004
01

AIR HOSTESS
PROMO

AIR HOSTESS
SINGLE CD1

26TH APRIL 2004
02

AIR HOSTESS
SINGLE CD2

26TH APRIL 2004
02

AIR HOSTESS
SINGLE 7"

26TH APRIL 2004
02

THUNDERBIRDS/3am
SINGLE CD1

26TH JULY 2004

3am/THUNDERBIRDS
SINGLE CD2

26TH JULY 2004

3am/THUNDERBIRDS
SINGLE DVD

26TH JULY 2004

A PRESENT FOR EVERYONE

The New Album. Out Now

Includes the hit singles **Crashed The Wedding,**
Who's David and **Air Hostess**

www. BUSTED .com